Photos by:
Demeter Balla: 20, 24
Imre Benkő: 43, 52
Lóránt Bérczi: 16, 47, 48, 66
László Csigó: 45, 55, 60, 61, 62, 63
Lajos Czeizing: 41, 50, 51
Endre Domonkos: 49
János Eifert: 12, 13, 15, 22, 23, 46
László Gyarmati: 2, 3, 4, 64, 65
Károly Hemző: 6, 7, 8, 18, 25, 30, 42, 53, 57, 67, 68
Tibor Inkey: 36, 38
Rudolf Járai: 44
Péter Korniss: 56
Sándor Kovács: 9, 40
Lajos Köteles: 29
dr. József Szabó: 10, 54, 58
Zsolt Szabóky: 1(front page), 21, 69, 71 (on the back)
Károly Szelényi: 5, 11
László Szelényi: 14, 27
János Szerencsés: 26, 28
Gyula Tahin: 17, 19, 31, 32, 33, 34, 35, 37, 39, 59
András Tokaji: 70

Translated by Lily Halápy
Translation revised by Jennifer Weighell

Design by Erzsébet Szabados

© Péter Dobai, 1980
ISBN 963 13 1043 4
Printed in Hungary, 1980
Dürer Printing House, Békéscsaba
CO 1870–h–8082

An old ferry, an old port, an old royal free borough–that was Budapest, Budapest's past dates back to the Roman Empire. This pearl of the Danube lies on both banks of the river, and, although it lies in the heart of the Continent, the far reaching Danube delta connects it with the sea. Originally it was three different towns–Óbuda (Old Buda), Buda and Pest, united in 1872 by the buoyant nineteenth century, a period fraught with utopias and hardship. Then subsequent decades imbued it with life and it grew into a metropolis: the capital, Budapest. As early as times preceding the Roman civilization the caves of Buda, the forests, so rich in timber and game, as well as the hot springs of the Buda hills attracted man to their gentle slopes near the bank of the river, and settlements were built. In to-

day's Óbuda, on the bank of the Danube Roman legions were stationed and it was there that Aquincum, the capital of the province of Pannonia Inferior, was built near their camps. The strong walls of Aquincum were finally demolished by the repeated attacks of the Great Migrations. In time the floods of the Danube covered the ruins with mud but archaeologists have unearthed the old paths, the buried atriums, the foundations of ancient castrums and now Roman Aquincum on the bank of the Danube is like a poem of archaeology in twentieth century Budapest. The ruins of amphitheatres–belonging to the most important establishments of Roman life–like robust mementoes of the culture of Antiquity stand even today in Óbuda. The tents of the Magyar chieftains who conquered the

present area of Hungary stood in the arenas of these amphitheatres over a thousand years ago. In the Middle Ages the urban status of Buda gradually grew, kings endowed it with the right to hold fairs and markets, and the right to operate ferries. After the devastations of the Mongolian invasion, the building of *Buda Castle* started (1247). Up to modern times its history has determined the life of merchants, craftsmen, wine and fruit-growers, who settled down in ever increasing numbers behind its bastions and walls. After a flourishing period during the Renaissance the town–and Buda Castle itself–was occupied by the Turks for a century and a half. During that time the country was severed from European development. In 1686 the united Christian forces succeeded in recapturing Buda

Castle from the Turks, whose empire was then in decline. A significant part of the medieval ruins of the Castle District were completely abolished during the long siege. At this time the characteristic Baroque features of the present day came into being. The nineteenth century which was a century of steamships and railways, saw the unification of Buda and Pest. Not only were bridges quickly built one after the other, but also the main roads and railway lines of Hungary and the neighbouring countries were constructed. Budapest, which is the capital not only of Hungary but of the Danube too, again rose from the ashes after the Second World War. When, in the spring of 1945, the cannon-fire had stopped, Budapest was in ruins, with all its bridges blown up and its people homeless. The city

was rebuilt, construction dominated destruction and the bridges reappeared. Present day Budapest is new districts full of housing estates.

Budapest is the city of the Danube, a city of bridges and islands. The river is an integral part of the city and is indeed its finest art monument. The most famous buildings of Budapest look out on to the Danube: on the eastern side Pest, here is the Parliament building, the Hungarian Academy of Sciences, the Parish Church of the Inner City (medieval in origin), and the Neo-Renaissance building of the University of Economics. On the western, the Buda side, there are several old medicinal baths and modern swimming pools, villas built on the terraced slopes of Rózsadomb (Rose Hill), and the Fishermen's Bastion on the rocky terrace of Castle Hill, Matthias Church, the Hilton Hotel, Buda Palace (the former royal palace), the Citadel on Gellért Hill, the imposing, *art nouveau* buildings of the Gellért Hotel and Medicinal Baths–all face the river. Budapest's charm is the Danube–the best approach is by boat. When one approaches Budapest from the North one sees the basilica of Esztergom, rising high above the banks, the ancient ruins of Visegrád castle, the dazzling scenery of the Danube Bend, the cathedral and the spires of the episcopal city of Vác, and the colourful roofs of Szentendre. One then comes across the wooded islands, seemingly uninhabited, and reaches the Roman Banks of Óbuda, with beaches, boathouses, avenues of poplars, and then further on is the misty silhouette of bridges, hills, spires

and domes of Budapest. The city has two nuclei and two voices: Buda on the hills and Pest on the plain. The visitor sees *one* city as when he looks down from Gellérthegy (Gellért Hill), Fishermen's Bastion, Hármashatárhegy (Three Boundary Hill) or the look-out tower on Jánoshegy (János Hill), he sees Budapest, but when he has made friends he knows there are two cities. Buda is on the slopes and terraces of hills and mountains—it is a *home* of the past. Pest covers a far larger area than Buda, as there are new housing estates on its plains and massive industrial districts to the north and south. Buda is Baroque and romantic, Pest is a metropolis. Pest hides its age, but the courtyards, the old houses, the ruins of city walls and dried out wells give it away. If we look at the union of the two

cities historically, Buda is more a royal town and Pest a bourgeois one. Buda has been preserved historically and architecturally as it was a royal residence. The Castle, palaces, monasteries, churches and meandering streets belong to centuries ago. Pest, larger in size with its boulevards, ringroads and avenues copes with present day traffic. The town of Pest shows signs of bourgeois virtues, of a careful and deliberate town planning. Buda is spectacular, and heroic, Pest is practical. Buda adapts to twentieth century life but twentieth century life must adapt to Buda. With its two opera houses, theatres, sport stadiums, art academies and universities Pest has taken over first place. Buda preserves the treasured past—the privilege of secrecy and remembrance and the quaintness

that awakens sorrow and nostalgia. A visitor walking up in the Castle District, among houses with medieval or baroque façades, musing among the beauty of vaults, which may seem to be purposeless, may imagine himself to be the child of another era. In Pest, however, the past and present overlap each other. Wherever a visitor is, he is the guest of an unforgettable city, which belongs to and speaks to the world.

Péter Dobai

2–4 The Danube Embankment of Buda
5 Buda panorama from Gellért Hill ▷

BUDAPEST

6 Roman tombstone in Aquincum
7 Aquincum.
Ruins of the civilian town
8 Turkish tombstones on Castle Hill

9 The southern barbican of Buda Castle
10 The Mace Tower

11 Buda Palace. The former royal palace on Castle Hill
12 The Matthias Fountain in the yard of Buda Palace

13 Detail of one of the Palace yards
14–15 In the Hungarian
National Gallery
16 The Gothic Hall of the Palace
(Museum of History)

17 Bécsikapu Square
18 Hilton Hotel

19 Copy of King Matthias's Beutzen
monument on the Gothic spire of
St. Nicolas' Church
20 Terrace of the Hilton Espresso

21 Fishermen's Bastion,
with the Parliament in the background ▷

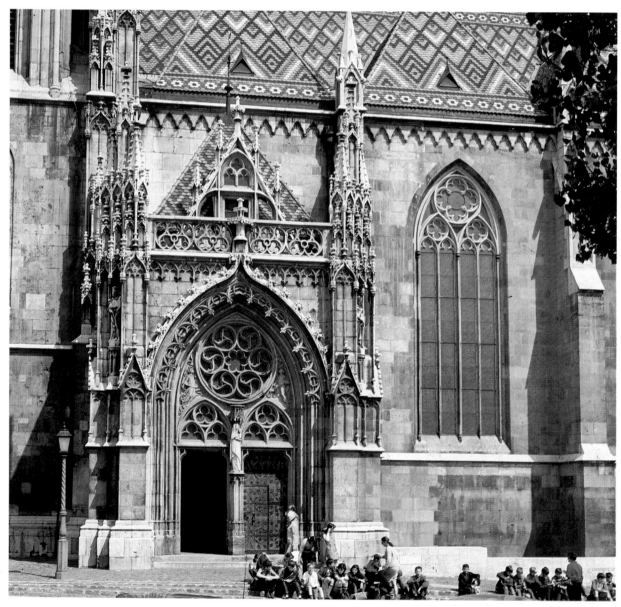

◁ 22–24 Matthias Church
◁ 25 Matthias Church

26 Országház Street
27 The Old Town Hall of Buda
on Szentháromság tér
28 Court of the Red Hedgehog House
(3 Hess András Square)

29 Front door of 25 Fortune Street
30 Gothic sitting niches in the gateway
of 13 Tárnok Street
31 Gothic sitting niches, 32 Uri Street
32 Courtyard of the house
No. 13 Dísz Square

33 6 Bécsikapu Square
34 14–16 Tárnok Street
35 12–14 Fortuna Street
36 Dárda Street

37 Biedermeier house with corner
turret, on the corner of Fő Street
and Pala Street
38 Detail of the Tabán area

39 Gül Baba Street on Rózsadomb
(Rose Hill)
40 Rococo house in Batthyány Square

◁ 41 The Chain Bridge (Lánchíd),
with Margaret Bridge and
Margaret Island in the background

42 Imre Varga's statue
of the nineteeth century dramatist
Imre Madách on Margaret Island

43 Underneath the trees of
Margaret Island

44 The old water tower on the Island ▷

45 The Chain Bridge
46 The Pest Abutment
of the Chain Bridge

47 Elisabeth Bridge (Erzsébet-híd)
and the Duna Intercontinental Hotel ▷

48 The Nereids' Fountain
before the Franciscan Church
49 Kossuth Lajos Street, with
the Parish Church of the Inner City
on the left

50–52 In Váci Street

53 The Danubius Fountain
in Engels Square
54 Vörösmarty Square

55 Façade of the building
No. 3. Martinelli Square
56 Petőfi Sándor Street

◁ 57 Kígyó Street
◁ 58 Felszabadulás Square
  seen from Párizsi udvar

59 Rákóczi Street
60–62 Buildings constructed
at the turn of the century
in Rákóczi Street and József körút

63 Népköztársaság útja
64 Building
with *art nouveau* decorations
in Ajtósi Dürer sor

65 Detail of the Millennial Monument
in Hősök tere (Heroes' Square)
66 Hősök tere

67 Miklós Ligeti's statue of Anonymus
(the anonymous chronicler
of King Béla III, 13th century)
68 The Pond in City Park with
Vajdahunyad Castle in the background

69 The Danube with Liberty Bridge
(Szabadság-híd) ▷

70 The Parliament Building seen
from Castle Hill